C000264940

TO:

_____

FROM:

_____

© 2014 Christian Art Gifts, RSA
Christian Art Gifts Inc., IL, USA

Designed by Christian Art Gifts

Images used under license from Shutterstock.com

Scripture quotations are taken from the *Holy Bible*,
New International Version® NIV®. Copyright © 1973, 1978, 1984, 2011
by International Bible Society. Used by permission of Biblica, Inc.®
All rights reserved worldwide.

Scripture quotations are taken from the *Holy Bible*,
New Living Translation®. Copyright © 1996, 2004, 2007
by Tyndale House Publishers, Inc., Carol Stream, Illinois 60188.
All rights reserved.

Scripture quotations are taken from the *Holy Bible*,
Contemporary English Version®.
Copyright © 1995 by American Bible Society.
All rights reserved.

Scripture quotations are taken from the New King James Version.
Copyright © 1979, 1980, 1982 by Thomas Nelson, Inc.
Used by permission. All rights reserved.

ISBN 978-1-4321-1249-3

Printed in China

18 19 20 21 22 23 24 25 26 27 – 13 12 11 10 9 8 7 6 5 4

Love

To love God is the greatest of virtues; to be loved by God is the greatest of blessings.

Anonymous

God demonstrates
His own love toward
us, in that while we
were still sinners,
Christ died for us.

Romans 5:8

I am a little pencil
in the hand of a
writing God, who
is sending a love
letter to the world.

Mother Teresa

We are more
than conquerors
through Him
who loved us.

Romans 8:37

God loves each of
us as if there were
only one of us.

St. Augustine

Give thanks to
the LORD for His
unfailing love.

Psalm 107:31

Of all earthly music,
that which reaches
farthest into heaven
is the beating of a
loving heart.

Henry Ward Beecher

I trust in Your
unfailing love;
my heart rejoices
in Your salvation.

Psalm 13:5

Love is like a
beautiful flower which
I may not touch,
but whose fragrance
makes the garden
a place of delight.

Helen Keller

As we live in God,
our love grows
more perfect …
Such love has no
fear, because
perfect love
expels all fear.

1 John 4:17-18

To love someone
is to show to them
their beauty,
their worth and
their importance.

Jean Vanier

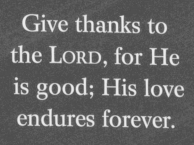

Give thanks to the LORD, for He is good; His love endures forever.

Psalm 118:29

Love is always
bestowed as a gift –
freely, willingly and
without expectation.
We don't love to be
loved; we love to love.

Leo Buscaglia

Sow righteousness
for yourselves,
reap the fruit of
unfailing love.

Hosea 10:12

Love is the sum
of all virtue,
and love disposes
us to good.

Jonathan Edwards

God causes
everything to
work together for
the good of those
who love Him.

Romans 8:28

Love attempts
what is above
its strength.

Thomas à Kempis

Your love,
LORD, reaches to
the heavens,
Your faithfulness
to the skies.

Psalm 36:5

Love is our
true destiny.
We do not find
the meaning
of life by ourselves
alone – we find
it with another.

Thomas Merton

Nothing in all
creation can separate
us from God's
love for us in
Christ Jesus our Lord!

Romans 8:39

Love is a symbol of
eternity. It wipes out
all sense of time,
destroying all
memory of a
beginning and all
fear of an end.

Anonymous

Love comes from God.

1 John 4:7

Since love
grows within you,
so beauty grows.
For love is the
beauty of the soul.

St. Augustine

Goodness and love will follow me all the days of my life, and I will dwell in the house of the LORD forever.

Psalm 23:6

Love gives life
purpose and
meaning.

Joyce Meyer

[Love] always
protects, always
trusts, always hopes,
always perseveres.

1 Corinthians 13:7

This is one of the
miracles of love:
It gives a power of
seeing through its
own enchantments
and yet not being
disenchanted.

C. S. Lewis

"The one who loves Me will be loved by My Father, and I too will love them and show Myself to them."

John 14:21

In this world,
there is no clarity.
There is only love
and action.

Mother Teresa

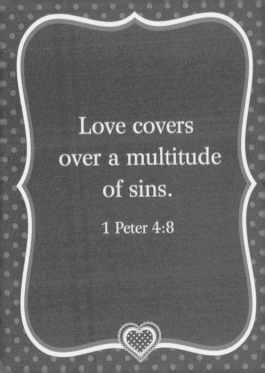

Love covers
over a multitude
of sins.

1 Peter 4:8

Nothing binds me
to my Lord like a
strong belief in
His changeless love.

Charles H. Spurgeon

These three remain:
faith, hope and love.
But the greatest of
these is love.

1 Corinthians 13:13

Love is not
affectionate feeling,
but a steady wish for
the loved person's
ultimate good as far
as it can be obtained.

C. S. Lewis

Love never fails.

1 Corinthians 13:8

There is no surprise more magical than the surprise of being loved. It is God's finger on man's shoulder.

Charles Morgan

The LORD appeared, saying, "I have loved you with an everlasting love; I have drawn you with unfailing kindness."

Jeremiah 31:3

A loving heart is
the beginning of
all knowledge.

Thomas Carlyle

If we love each other,
God lives in us, and
His love is brought to
full expression in us.

1 John 4:12

Love makes
the music of the
blest above,
heaven's harmony
is universal love.

William Cowper

God's love has been poured into our hearts through the Holy Spirit, who has been given to us.

Romans 5:5

Though our feelings
come and go, God's
love for us does not.

C. S. Lewis

You, Lord, are a
compassionate
and gracious God,
abounding in love
and faithfulness.

Psalm 86:15

To love abundantly
is to live abundantly,
and to love forever
is to live forever.

Henry Drummond

Love the LORD your
God with all your
heart and with all
your soul and with all
your strength.

Deuteronomy 6:5

God's love
is unconditional.
Be sure that
yours is too!

The Lord is good
and His love
endures forever;
His faithfulness
continues through
all generations.

Psalm 100:5

Love is the
energy of life.

Robert Browning

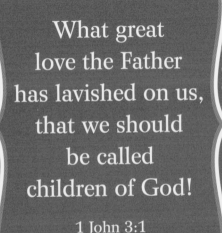

What great
love the Father
has lavished on us,
that we should
be called
children of God!

1 John 3:1

The best use of
life is love. The best
expression of love
is time. The best
time to love is now.

Rick Warren

Walk in the way
of love, just as Christ
loved us and gave
Himself up for us as a
fragrant offering and
sacrifice to God.

Ephesians 5:2

Love is the only
force capable of
transforming an
enemy into a friend.

Martin Luther King, Jr.

This is love:
not that we loved
God, but that He
loved us and sent
His Son as an
atoning sacrifice
for our sins.

1 John 4:10

Faith goes up
the stairs that love
has built and
looks out of the
windows which
hope has opened.

Charles H. Spurgeon

The LORD is compassionate and merciful, slow to get angry and filled with unfailing love.

Psalm 103:8

Love is the river
of life in the world.

Henry Ward Beecher

God so loved the
world that He gave
His one and only
Son, that whoever
believes in Him shall
not perish but have
eternal life.

John 3:16

Love is an image
of God, and not
a lifeless image, but
the living essence
of the divine nature
which beams full
of all goodness.

Martin Luther

God's love and
kindness will
shine upon us like
the sun that rises
in the sky.

Luke 1:78

When there is love
in the home, there is
joy in the heart.

Anonymous

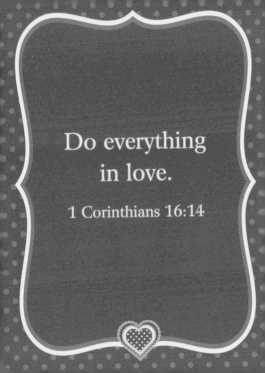

Do everything
in love.

1 Corinthians 16:14

The highest proof
of the spirit is love.
Love the eternal
thing which can
already on earth
possess as it really is.

Albert Schweitzer

Love is patient,
love is kind. It does
not envy, it does not
boast, it is not proud.

1 Corinthians 13:4

Our love to God is measured by our everyday fellowship with others and the love it displays.

Andrew Murray

The LORD your God is living among you. With His love, He will calm all your fears. He will rejoice over you with joyful songs.

Zephaniah 3:17

However devoted
you are to God,
you may be sure that
He is immeasurably
more devoted to you.

Meister Eckhart

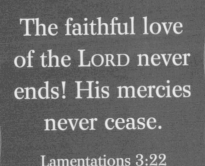

The faithful love
of the LORD never
ends! His mercies
never cease.

Lamentations 3:22

Faith makes all
things possible ...
love makes all
things easy.

Dwight L. Moody

"Though the
mountains be
shaken and the hills
be removed, yet My
unfailing love for you
will not be shaken,"
says the LORD.

Isaiah 54:10

Love is something
more stern and
splendid than
mere kindness.

C. S. Lewis

Whoever pursues
righteousness
and unfailing
love will find life,
righteousness,
and honor.

Proverbs 21:21

I never knew
how to worship
until I knew
how to love.

Henry Ward Beecher

Let love and faithfulness never leave you; bind them around your neck, write them on the tablet of your heart.

Proverbs 3:3

To love
someone means
to see them as God
intended them.

Fyodor Dostoevsky

You, Lord,
are forgiving and
good, abounding
in love to all who
call to You.

Psalm 86:5

Fundamental
to every emotion
of love to Christ is
trust in Christ.

Alexander MacLaren

The LORD loves righteousness and justice; the earth is full of His unfailing love.

Psalm 33:5

He that
dwelleth in love,
dwelleth in God.
God is love.

Henry Drummond

Give thanks
to the LORD, for He
is good; His love
endures forever.

1 Chronicles 16:34

Love alone makes heavy burdens light and bears in equal balance things pleasing and displeasing. Love makes bitter things tasteful and sweet.

Thomas à Kempis

Know that the LORD
your God is God;
He is the faithful God,
keeping His covenant
love to those who
love Him.

Deuteronomy 7:9

Love seeks one
thing only: the good
of the one loved.
It leaves all the other
secondary effects to take
care of themselves.
Love, therefore,
is its own reward.

Thomas Merton

Love your
neighbor as
yourself.

Leviticus 19:18

The chains of love
are stronger than
the chains of fear.

William Gurnall

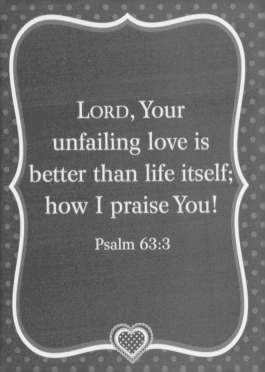

LORD, Your
unfailing love is
better than life itself;
how I praise You!

Psalm 63:3

Dwell in love,
and then you
dwell in God.

William Law

This is how we
know what love is:
Jesus Christ laid
down His life for us.

1 John 3:16

Divine love is perfect
peace and joy, it is
a freedom from all
disquiet, it is all
content and
happiness; and
makes everything
to rejoice in itself.

William Law

Above all, clothe yourselves with love, which binds us all together in perfect harmony.

Colossians 3:14

Love is the only
fire that is hot
enough to melt
the iron
obstinacy of a
creature's will.

Alexander MacLaren

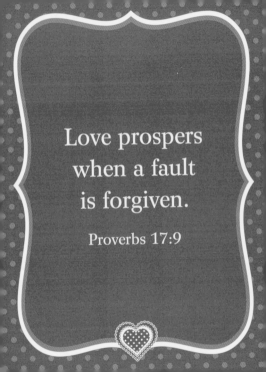

Love prospers
when a fault
is forgiven.

Proverbs 17:9

Love deems
this world worth
rescuing.

Philip Yancey

God is love,
and all who live in
love live in God, and
God lives in them.

1 John 4:16